Bend Brews

A Beer Lover's Guide to Bend Area Breweries

André Bartels & Bob Woodward

Bend Brews

A Beer Lover's Guide to Bend Area Breweries

First Edition

For all inquiries contact us at bendbrews.photomotif.com.

Printed in the United States

Text by Bob Woodward

Design and layout by André Bartels with creative support from Braden Brook (www.roundedcorner.com)

All photos by the authors except otherwise noted

First published 2010 by André Bartels and Bob Woodward, Bend, Oregon

ISBN: 978-1-4507-3297-0

Contents

Introduction

Twenty-three years ago; Gary Fish opened the Deschutes Brewery and Public House in downtown Bend, Central Oregon's first microbrewery and brewpub. He hardly could have imagined at that time that craft brewing and craft beers would one day play an important role in Central Oregon's economy and everyday life.

Today, Fish's Deschutes Brewery is Oregon's largest craft brewer. Such tasteful success has opened the door for many, small local brewers to serve beer enthusiasts around Bend and the larger community. Each brewer's beers are available at their own distinct pubs and tasting rooms, as well as at local and regional cafes, restaurants, and taverns.

"What makes Bend brews special," notes Chris Justema of Cascade Lakes Brewing, "is that all the brewers make really good beer. What makes the local brewpub scene so special is that locals support all of us equally."

Bend as Beer Heaven? You bet. With that in mind, pick up a Bend Ale Trail™ Passport and Map (see page 42) and start a tour of some wonderful establishments. You'll meet some great people and enjoy some of the best in locally handcrafted beers you'll find anywhere.

Enjoy your pub crawl, Bend, and Central Oregon.

Cheers,

André Bartels & Bob Woodward

Acknowledgments

Thanks to all the brewers and brewpub owners for their time and patience, Visit Bend for their support, Dennis Hanson and Nick Guistina for their editing skills, and our strong livers for getting us through this task.

Some Microbrew History

An abbreviated Bartels/Woodward history of modern craft brewing and Central Oregon brewers.

1960: Lawrence Steese buys San Francisco's historic (founded in 1896) Anchor Brewing and continues a long tradition of Anchor Steam® beer. The beer is served in a small brown-bag lunch area at the brewery and in a few local restaurants.

Courtesy of Anchor Brewing, San Francisco

Anchor on Russian Hill ca. 1905/06

1965: Steese plans to close Anchor Brewing when Stanford grad Fritz Maytag steps in and buys it. Maytag turns Anchor Steam® into a much sought-after craft beer.

1974: Portlander Mike McMenamin and friends open the Produce Row Café. The cafe serves only tasty imports, thereby awakening the imagination and palate of Portland-area beer lovers to the wider world of uniquely crafted beers.

1970s: The Campaign for Real Ale (CAMRA) movement in the United Kingdom starts a trend away from public houses doing business exclusively with mega-breweries. Instead, pub owners look to smaller "craft" brewers for high-quality lagers and ales to serve their clientele.

1979: Chuck Coury opens The Cartwright in Portland. Oregon's first pub serving locally made beer, the Cartwright doesn't survive, but it sets the stage for brewpubs to follow.

1982: Scotsman Bert Grant takes the craft brewing and brewpub idea to Washington State, opening Grant's Brewery Pub in Yakima. Grant's old-country influence will be felt in the craft brewing business for years to come.

1983: Brian and Mike McMenamin open their Hillsdale Pub brewpub in Portland. It serves a variety of hand-crafted beers.

1984: Successful Oregon winemakers Richard and Nancy Ponzi establish the Columbia River Brewery (later renamed BridgePort) in Portland.

1985: Oregon law is amended so that beer can be made on the same location where it's sold. This sets into motion a brewpub revolution.

1986: The Widmer brothers, Rob and Kurt, introduce their Hefeweizen. It becomes an instant classic among the craft brew faithful and attracts people new to craft brewing.

Courtesy of Widmer Brothers Brewing

Rob and Kurt Widmer in the early days

1988: The Full Sail Brewing Company begins making craft beers in Hood River.

Then craft brewing migrates over the mountains and up from the Columbia River Basin to Central Oregon

1988: Gary Fish launches the Deschutes Brewery and Public House in Bend.

Courtesy of Deschutes Brewery

Gary Fish pours beer in the Bend Public House

1994: Cascade Lakes Brewing starts making beer in Redmond. Two years later, its 7th Street Brew House begins business in that city.

1995: The Bend Brewing Company opens its brewpub on Bend's Brooks Street.

2000: Tyler Reichert starts brewing Silver Moon beer at his home brewers supply company. In 2005, he opens his current brewpub and brewery close to the heart of downtown Bend.

2004: Cascade Lakes opens its Lodge on Bend's west side.

2004: McMenamins unveils its Old St. Francis School brewpub and lodging establishment near the heart of downtown Bend.

Courtesy of McMenamins

The Old St. Francis School in Bend in the 1940s

2006: 10 Barrel Brewing Company (known then as Wildfire Brewing Company) is incorporated. Brewing starts in earnest in 2007 and a Bend brewpub is opened in the spring of 2010.

2008: The Three Creeks Brewery is established in Sisters.

2010: Boneyard Beer commences production in Bend's Old Town neighborhood on the Cinco de Mayo holiday.

2011: GoodLife Brewing Company starts construction on its brewery and begins brewing operations.

2011: Old Mill Brew Wërks starts brewing.

10 Barrel Brewing Company

1135 NW Galveston Ave
Bend, OR 97701

Chris Cox, Jeremy Cox, Garrett Wales

The 10 Barrel Brewing Company began making and distributing craft beer throughout Central Oregon in 2007, originally under the Wildfire Brewing Company name. But Garrett Wales, Chris Cox and Jeremy Cox, the company's three partners, really wanted to open a brewpub. And they were picky. "We wanted a place," says Garrett Wales, "where we could have a huge patio and roll-up garage doors that connected the inside of the pub to the outside and the patio."

Their search went on until 2009 when the trio came across a former bakery building on Bend's west side. "The minute we checked it out," Wales recalls, "we knew it was what we wanted." Within days of seeing the place, a deal was struck and work begun on turning the building into a pub.

Opened in February of 2010, the 10 Barrel brewpub proved an instant hit in part because of its sleek, minimalist interior décor, a bar that opens to the outside and a 1,400 square-foot paver-stone patio. A patio that's the site of the popular "Beats on The Bricks" Sunday music series during the warm weather months.

A Unique Brewpub

To enhance the pub's unique character, every piece of pub furniture from the chairs to the tables, benches, and even the bar, was created by local craftsmen. The metal tables on the patio are, for example, the handiwork of a craftsman who lives and creates close to the brewpub.

The three partners cite a background in the restaurant and bar-service business as key in their decision to open a brewery and brewpub. The Coxes own JC's Bar and Grill in downtown Bend, while Wales grew up working in his father's local liquor-distribution business.

The Cox brothers also found inspiration from the McMenamin brothers when the two craft brew legends were revamping the Old St. Francis School into a pub and lodging establishment. The McMenamin brothers frequented JC's after a day's work on their nearby property and over pints they influenced the Coxes to get into the craft brewing business.

Pairing Food with Beer

As they moved ahead on opening their brewpub, the 10 Barrel partners were adamant about the food they'd serve. "Pizza for sure," states Wales," and to keep it simple with a somewhat limited menu of very tasty food. We don't employ a cook; we employ a chef."

As to the beer, the following are always on tap: District 10 Pale Ale, S1NISTOR Black Ale, Apocalypse IPA, and Northwest Red. Seasonal brews include an Oatmeal Stout and a Belgian Blonde, which are rotated in and out with other beers. Some of the offerings on tap are kept under nitro for a smoother, richer-textured taste. 10 Barrel's best-seller is the Apocalypse IPA followed by the District 10 Pale Ale.

A new brewing facility contains a 50-barrel system and will allow for more beers in 22-ounce bottles and expansion of the brand beyond Oregon.

"Within days of seeing the place, a deal was struck and work begun on turning the building into a pub."

10 BARREL BREWING CO.

10 BARREL BREWING CO.

Location	**Brewery** 20750 High Desert Lane #107 Bend, OR 97701 **Brewpub** 1135 NW Galveston Ave Bend, OR 97701
Established	2007
Founder/Owner	Garrett Wales, Chris & Jeremy Cox
Brewmaster(s)	Jimmy Seifrit
Web site	www.10barrel.com
Phone	Brewery: 541.585.1007 Brewpub: 541.678.5228
Standard Beers	Summer Ale District 10 Pale Ale S1NISTOR Black Ale Apocalypse IPA Northwest Red
Seasonal Beers	Belgian Blonde Coffee Porter Duke Pray for Snow Strong Ale Oatmeal Stout Double Woody O'Reilly's Irish Red ISA

BEERS ON TAP

	%	IBU'S
Belgian Dubbel	7.3	26
District 10 Pale Ale	5.3	41
1nistor Black Ale	5.4	28
'Pocalypse IPA	6.5	65
'Rileys Irish Red Ale	4.4	26
Vitro - See Server		
O Barrel Summer Ale	4.7	26

Bend Brewing Company

1019 NW Brooks Street
Bend, OR 97701

Wendi Day

From the day it opened in 1995, Bend Brewing Company became instantly popular and quickly known as Bend's go-to, family-friendly pub. "Our family-friendly reputation happened organically," says co-owner Wendi Day, who with Terry Standly started the brewpub with the simple mission of offering "great food and award-winning beers."

Today, the spacious, airy brewpub just off the banks of the Deschutes River is a thriving destination, not only with families and locals, but also with tourists due to its enticing beer/food mix and proximity to downtown Bend's action.

An Award-Winning Brewmaster

The beer side of Bend Brewing's winning food/beverage equation started with the arrival of brewmaster Tonya Cornett in 2002. A graduate of the World Brewing Academy and holder of an international diploma in brewing technology, Cornett was the first female ever to be named Champion Brewer by the Brewers Association World Beer Cup group in 2008. That same year, Bend Brewing took home the award as the "Best Small Brewery in The World."

Cornett oversees brewing of 1,000 barrels of beer per year, the majority of which is sold on the brewpub's premises with local distribution to some 20 other pubs and taverns. There are five standard beers on tap at the brewpub at all times: High Desert Hefeweizen, Metolius Golden Ale, Elk Lake India Pale Ale, Outback Old Ale, and Pinnacle Porter. Of those, Elk Lake IPA is the top seller. Seasonal brews are also offered. Among them are Hop-Head, Imperial IPA, Paulina Pale Ale, and Bohemian Pilsner. An Artist Series of bottle labels features local art work.

Keeping it Small

"We've purposely kept things small," Day says of the brewing operations," and it's paid off in quality." Staying small has created a close-knit, almost familial relationship among the brewpub's 33

employees. "We have a good time and all work together well," Day indicates, "the camaraderie here is terrific."

Such morale even enlivens patrons who frequent the pub. The place is always bustling with activity that's made more enjoyable by the friendly server staff.

On a summer day, you can sit outdoors and enjoy being close to the river running close by. Come winter, you can sit and relax indoors and watch the snow fly and the geese wing-in to land on the nearby water.

Enhanced with good food and splendid quaff, the view from the Bend Brewing Company is good any time of the year.

"Our family-friendly reputation happened organically."

Location	**Brewery & Brewpub**
	1019 NW Brooks Street
	Bend, OR 97701
Established	1995
Founder/Owner	Wendi Day, Terry Standly
Brewmaster(s)	Tonya Cornett
Web site	www.bendbrewingco.com
Phone	Brewery: 541.383.1599
Standard Beers	High Desert Hefeweizen
	Metolius Golden Ale
	Elk Lake IPA
	Outback Old Ale
	Pinnacle Porter
Seasonal Beers	Big Eddy Bitter
	Paulina Pale Ale
	Hop-Head Imperial IPA

Boneyard Beer

37 NW Lake Place, Suite B
Bend, OR 97701

Anthony Lawrence, Melodee Storey, Clay Storey

Take a brewer with serious craft-brewing industry cred (Anthony Lawrence), put him together with a husband-and-wife team (Clay and Melodee Storey) who are 20-year veterans of the construction business, and you have the beginnings of Boneyard Beer.

Lawrence's craft-brewing resume includes a stint as a brewer at Deschutes Brewing, starting in 1988. He leaves the brewery as a senior brewer in 2001, embarking on a nomadic life traveling nationwide to build microbreweries.

First stop, Rio Salado in Tempe, Arizona, where he brews traditional German lagers and pilsners. Several more stops along the way and he ends up working at what many consider one the finest craft brewers in the U.S. — Firestone Walker Brewing in Paso Robles, California.

Eventually tiring of working for others, Lawrence leaves Firestone Walker to form his own microbrew-industry consulting company called Brewtal.

Collecting Equipment

"Through Brewtal," Lawrence recalls, "I developed my welding skills and started to salvage a lot of retired beer-making equipment from various brewers' 'boneyards' and hauled it back to Bend." Hence,

the new brewery's name.

Much of that equipment came from the Three Floyds Brewery located in Indiana, just outside Chicago.

Lawrence builds up a stockpile of beer-making gear at his Bend home and starts looking for a place to set it up and begin brewing.

Enter the Storeys who own a commercial space that Lawrence wants to rent. Taken by Lawrence and his brewery plans and needing a change from the construction business, the Storeys ask, as Clay Storey puts it, "to make a dream happen."

The Grand Opening

They join forces and open Boneyard Beer on May 5, 2010 making three beers: Bone-A-Fide Pale Ale, Black 13, and a cherry/wheat beer called Girl Beer. Girl Beer is a unique, bubbly, light beer, more of, as Lawrence states, "a beermosa."

Now the brewery makes eight beers, all of which are available

daily at Boneyard's tasting room (Wednesday night is the very popular growler night) and at several bars and restaurants in Bend and across Oregon.

Boneyard is expanding the brand up and down the coast with production of up to 4,500 barrels per year and two brews (RPM IPA and Girl) coming in cans.

There will also be, "all sorts of fun ideas from Flemish sour browns to Belgian-style beers," according to Lawrence, who adds, "We have the ability to do one-off brews very easily."

"We have the ability to do one-off brews very easily."

Location	**Brewery & Tasting Room** 37 NW Lake Place, Suite B Bend, OR 97701
Established	2010
Founder/Owner	Anthony Lawrence, Clay & Melodee Storey
Brewmaster(s)	Anthony Lawrence
Web site	www.boneyardbeer.com
Phone	541.323.2325
Standard Beers	Bone-A-Fide Pale Ale Black 13 Girl Beer RPM IPA
Seasonal Beers	Diablo Rojo Armored Fist Wit Shack Wit Hop Venom IPA

Cascade Lakes Brewing

1441 SW Chandler Street
Bend, OR 97702

"We wanted our Lodge pub/restaurant on Bend's west side to be a place where skiers and cyclists could go to on their way home or to their overnight accommodations and talk about their days on the slopes, roads, or trails over a beer and some food," says Chris Justema, who along with Ron Kutella, owns Cascade Lakes Brewing. "We like to see cycling cleats and ski pants in The Lodge."

The Lodge has a ski resort feel to it with a large family dining section and cozy bar warmed by a shared fireplace. There's also a loft area with a pool table and dart boards.

A Place for Outdoor Enthusiasts

The idea of having such a space for locals and tourists who are active outdoor sports enthusiasts is rooted in the success of Cascade Lakes' first property—the 7th Street Brew House in Redmond. Just off Highway 97 on the way to and from Smith Rock State Park and Lake Billy Chinook, 7th Street has attracted rock climbers and water skiers since 1996. Today, the brewery's Monkey Face Porter honors the climbers, while the Rooster Tail Ale pays tribute to water skiers and wake boarders.

Two years prior to setting up the Redmond pub, Cascade Brewing

Chris Justema

opened its brewery on Redmond's eastside.

The original brewery started making beer with primitive dairy equipment. Time and demands for more production led to the present-day, state-of-the-art, custom built 25-barrel brewing operation featuring 12- and 22-ounce bottling lines, a full-service lab, as well as advanced malt handling equipment.

Cascade Lakes brews 4,500 barrels a year and features eight standard and 10 seasonal brews. It offers 12-ounce six-packs and three-packs of 22-ounce beers, both comprised of a variety of beers. "We use the 22-ounce three-packs," says Justema, "to showcase some of the more interesting beers we make."

Speaking of interesting, Cascade Lakes brews also stand out for

their distinctive, fun labels, a collaborative effort of Justema and Bend freelance-designer Casey Davis.

Managing Growth

Cascade Lakes' beers are currently distributed throughout Oregon and Southwest Washington. Plans call for increased distribution into Washington and Idaho.

While expanding the brand, Cascade Lakes has also focused on upgrading its holdings. For example, the 7th Street Brew House was completely rebuilt in 2004 and now includes a small brew operation.

Smiling as he pours out a draft at The Lodge, Justema laughs, "On the brew side of our operations, we make what we like to drink and sell the remainder. On the other side, we just happen to be a hospitality-based company that's in the business of brewing beer."

"We like to see cycling cleats and ski pants in The Lodge."

CASCADE LAKES BREWING COMPANY

Location
Brewery
2141 SW 1st Street
Redmond, OR 97756
7th Street Brew House
855 7th Street
Redmond, OR 97756
The Lodge
1441 SW Chandler Ave
Bend, OR 97702

Established 1994

Founder/Owner Chris Justema, Ron Kutella

Brewmaster(s) John Van Duzer

Web site www.cascadelakes.com

Phone Brewery: 541.923.3110
7th Street : 541.923.1795
The Lodge: 541.388.4998

Standard Beers Blonde Bombshell
Rooster Tail Ale
Monkey Face Porter
Pine Marten Pale Ale
20" Brown
I.P.A.
Angus MacDouglas

Seasonal Beers Harvest Ale Fresh Hop
Skookum Creek Ale
Paulina Lake Pilsner
Runaway Imperial IPA
Kölsch
Bald Mountain Bock
Riverside Red
Santa's Little Helper
Waist Deep Weiss

Deschutes Brewery

1044 NW Bond Street
Bend, OR 97701

When Gary Fish departed Salt Lake City for Bend in 1987, he planned to use his experience in the restaurant business to open a local pub that combined good food and craft beers. "I hoped that the concept would prove successful," Fish says, "because I wanted to stay and enjoy the Central Oregon lifestyle—skiing, fishing, and playing golf-on my off-hours."

Fish opened the Deschutes Brewery and Public House in downtown Bend on June 27, 1988. His timing would appear flawed given the fact that Bend's economy was just starting to crawl out of a long depression.

But as a sign that better times might indeed be on the way, the brewpub was an immediate hit with Bend locals. Coincidentally, the nascent craft-brewing business was beginning a meteoric rise in popularity with Portland area pub-goers and this was causing ripples throughout the national community of tavern owners and brewers. Within months of its opening, Deschutes Brewery had to increase production in direct response to requests for its beers from Oregon tavern and bar owners who had sampled the brewery's beers while visiting Bend. "Orders started coming in," Fish says, "and our first pallet of beer destined for an out-of-town tavern departed Bend on the top of a truck loaded with recycled cardboard."

Gary Fish

Courtesy of Deschutes Brewery/Photo by Holland Studios

Business ramped up quickly after that first shipment. By 1993, having outgrown its brewing operation in the downtown pub, ground was broken on a new brewery building overlooking the Deschutes River on Bend's west side.

The Largest Craft Brewer in Oregon

Today, Deschutes Brewing has 110,000 square-feet of production and warehousing space in Bend. With all that space and increased beer production, Deschutes is arguably the largest craft brewer in Oregon, producing 200,000 barrels of beer annually for distribution in 50 states.

Want to sip on a Mirror Pond Pale Ale while watching a Major League Baseball spring training game in Arizona? Now you can;

just as easily as you can at Deschutes' now three-year-old pub in Portland's Pearl District.

Back when things got started in the '80s, the brewery offered a light, medium, and dark trio of beers: Cascade Golden Ale, Bachelor Bitter, and Black Butte Porter. Today, it offers 16 beers during any given year, with Mirror Pond Pale Ale the brand's top seller. In fact, Deschutes Brewery's original Black Butte Porter is today the number one selling porter in the country.

Rooted in Bend

While Deschutes plans to expand its national distribution and grow its production space yet again to accommodate increased demand for its product, the brewery remains Bend-centric when it comes to largesse. "Giving back to the community," says Fish, "is part of our culture, our company's DNA." So important is generosity and custodianship that the brewery has an established community-involvement committee.

Road and mountain bike cycling are just two of the local community's active groups that the Deschutes Brewery has helped foster and support through sponsorships. What began with sponsoring the Cascade Cycling Classic, America's oldest ongoing road cycling race, grew into the brewery's primary sponsorship and hosting of the 2009 and 2010 National Cyclo-Cross Championships on Deschutes Brewery property. Local mountain bike races and trail maintenance events also are part of the brewery's dedication to service.

Ride a bike over to the Deschutes Brewery and take one of its regularly scheduled tours. Then cycle downtown to the original public house which is being expanded to better serve customers. Now that's a day well spent.

Location	**Brewery**
	901 SW Simpson Ave
	Bend, OR 97702
	Bend Public House
	1044 NW Bond Street
	Bend, OR 97701
Established	1988
Founder/Owner	Gary Fish
Brewmaster(s)	Larry Sidor
Web site	www.deschutesbrewery.com
Phone	Brewery: 541.385.8606
	Public House: 541.382.9242
Standard Beers	Black Butte Porter
	Mirror Pond Pale Ale
	Inversion IPA
	Obsidian Stout
	Green Lakes Organic Ale
	Cascade Ale
	Bachelor ESB
Seasonal Beers	Red Chair NWPA
	Twilight Ale
	Jubelale

McMenamins Old St. Francis School

700 NW Bond Street
Bend, OR 97701

Brian and Mike McMenamin

In the short history of Oregon's craft-brewing business, the McMenamin brothers, Brian and Mike, have played remarkable roles. They've also been the driving force behind the refurbishing of historic buildings (nearly 60 throughout the Northwest) and repurposing them as pubs with lodging and entertainment venues.

The rebirth of Bend's St. Francis School is a classic example of the McMenamin brothers' playful creativity. Bend's first parochial school, it now offers lodging and food as well as beer brewed on the premises. Unique amenities like the movie theater and the luxurious soaking pool make the Old St. Francis School unique among Bend's popular hostelries.

Looking for a Place in Bend

"We'd been looking for a place in Bend for a long time," recalls Brian McMenamin, "and when we found the St. Francis School, we loved the fact that it was historical, a part of the downtown area, and deeply integrated into the community since 1936."

The school's history dates even further back to the 1920s when Father Luke Sheehan, a missionary from County Cork, Ireland, began his quest to open a school for Bend's Catholic children. His dream

was realized in 1936 with the construction of St. Francis School on Bend's Bond Street.

The original school building's classrooms now serve as the Old St. Francis School's main restaurant and pub. Downstairs, in what used to be the music and preschool rooms, are the brewing operations.

The schoolhouse's south wing, built in 1953 and expanded in 1960 to accommodate more classrooms, today houses 19 guest rooms with full baths.

Across a courtyard, offering plenty of places to sit outdoors, the former parish hall (built in 1968 to serve as the school's gym), now houses a small pub, movie theater, meeting rooms, and soaking pool.

On the property's east side, a number of bungalows welcome large family gatherings, receptions, and extended stays.

The Historic Theme

As with all McMenamins' establishments, the Old St. Francis School is packed with antique furniture, posters, signage, architectural elements and lighting fixtures, as well as old photographs and interpretive plaques detailing the property's history.

Tim Hills, McMenamins' full-time historian, creates the historical displays. The antiques, old signs and unique touches such as stained glass windows are those of Mike McMenamin.

With site history and period motif, McMenamins also manifests traditional excellence in brewing. And if the beers aren't temptation enough, Old St. Francis School's hearty menu will keep you coming back through the school house doors.

"When we found the St. Francis School, we loved the fact that it was historical, a part of the downtown area, and deeply integrated into the community since 1936."

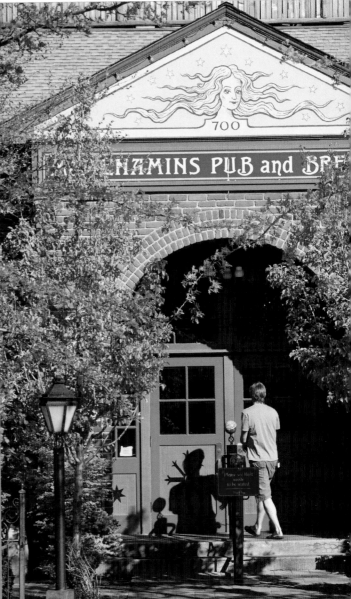

Location	**Brewery and Brewpub** 700 NW Bond Street Bend, OR 97701
Established	2004
Founder/Owner	Brian and Mike McMenamin
Brewmaster(s)	Mike White
Web site	www.mcmenamins.com
Phone	541.382.5174
Standard Beers	Hammerhead Ale Ruby Ale Terminator Stout Sunflower IPA Cascade Head Crystal Ale Bagdad Ale Edgefield Wheat Nebraska Bitter Black Rabbit Porter
Seasonal Beers	Irish Stout Workingman's Red Copper Moon Sleepy Hollow Nut Brown Kris Kringle

Silver Moon Brewing

**24 NW Greenwood Ave.
Bend, OR 97701**

It's not often that a brewer's story begins with a stint as a forester in Vermont. Yet that's how Silver Moon Brewing owner Tyler Reichert's career in craft brewing began.

"I was managing a forest in the northern part of the state and lived in an old farmhouse deep inside the property," Reichert says, "and living there required me to haul in all the household essentials by foot."

After tasting a friend's home brew, one of those Reichert loads into his farmhouse included all the ingredients for making home brew. Soon Reichert was treating his fellow foresters to the results of his own brewing efforts.

In making his own brew, Reichert kept harking back to an amber ale he'd tried a few years before in a Burlington, Vermont pub. "It was the 'ah-ha' moment. Drinking that amber just hit me, and I wanted to make something like it."

Moving West

Tiring of forestry work in Vermont, Reichert headed West looking for work and to ski. His route led to stops in Missoula, Montana, and Jackson, Wyoming, before arriving in Bend in 1998.

Tyler Reichert

After a few odd jobs in local forestry, he decided to try something new. That turned out to be crafting beer. In 1998, he bought a home-brewers supply business. A year later, he obtained his brewing license and started making his own beers, selling them at his shop and then at a few local pubs.

"I purchased all the beer-making equipment from a defunct brewing operation in Bandon on the Oregon Coast," he notes, "and on the way home, coming over the final rise on Highway 138 on an icy roadway, I looked up at the brilliant crescent moon in the sky and thanked it for serving as the guiding light, getting me and my cargo home safely.

"It was at that moment that I decided to call my brewery Silver Moon, not only for the moon that night, but also for the ones we see every month over the Oregon High Desert region."

In 2005, Reichert moved his businesses (he would soon sell the home-brewing supply operation) into the brewery's current

home on Greenwood Avenue. Silver Moon's new quarters previously housed an antiques store that, over the next five years, Reichert transformed into a brewery and pub specializing in brews, a diverse pub food menu, and music.

Adding Music to the Beer

"I love listening to live music," Reichert said, "and when I had my small store and brewery operation, I had a bluegrass band use the space for practice. Not long afterward, I put a note on my outside reader-board inviting bands to use my space to practice. They did."

So the idea of adding music at the new Silver Moon locale was always there foremost. "Then when the number of Bend venues for live music started to dwindle," Reichert points out, "I jumped at the chance to offer musicians a place to play for live audiences."

Now the pub offers a regular schedule of performances from acoustic bluegrass groups to newgrass, indie, roots, and pure folk ensembles.

With the addition of live music as well as some live theater, Silver Moon is now considered a prime performance space in Bend. It's also noted as a true "locals" place with an unpretentious, unhurried atmosphere.

"I've always taken the lead from my customers as to what they want in a pub," Reichert states, "and they want someplace that's not fancy, but comfortable and one that serves great food and beer."

As to what drives him to continue to make craft brews, Reichert says, "life is short, so why not make and drink good beer."

Silver Moon
BREWING · BEND, OR

Location	Brewery and Taproom
	24 NW Greenwood Ave.
	Bend, OR 97701
Established	2000
Founder/Owner	Tyler Reichert
Brewmaster(s)	Tyler West
Web site	www.silvermoonbrewing.com
Phone	541.388.8331

Standard Beers
Bridge Creek Pilsner
Hounds Tooth Amber
Snake Bite Porter
Badlands Bitter
Hop Knob IPA

Seasonal Beers
Dark Side Stout
Spring Head Kölsch
Bock Joy!
Hop Fury IPA
Winter Moon Stron Ale
Hoptagon Imperial IPA
Epic Trail Ale

Three Creeks Brewing Co.

721 Desperado Court
Sisters, OR 97759

As his involvement in an e-commerce venture in Phoenix, Arizona, wound down, Wade Underwood thought about opening a brewery and brewpub. After all, he'd been in love with the idea for years and Phoenix was short of such places.

Then on the umpteenth day of incredible Arizona summer heat, Underwood decided it was time to move his dream somewhere else. That turned out to be the Northwest which, in turn, became Sisters, Oregon.

"When I moved here," Underwood says, "I wanted to add value to the community, and a local pub that made its own brew and served tasty food proved to be that."

The First Brewery for Sisters

Opened in July 2008, Three Creeks Brewing quickly gained a reputation for its food and beer, as well as for its location close to the increasingly popular Peterson Ridge trail system for mountain bikers, hikers, and runners. The brewery also proved a hit with skiers on their way to and from Mount Bachelor and Hoodoo ski areas.

Wade Underwood

The brewing operation has recently been expanded to a 20-barrel system. Most of that output is consumed at the brewpub with limited distribution going to restaurants and taverns in Central Oregon and Portland.

Six standard beers are always available. They are Knotty Blond, Anvil Amber, Stonefly Rye, Firestorm Red, Hoodoo Voodoo, and Old Prospector.

Counting four from the brewery's stable menu of 12 seasonal beers yields a total of 10 on tap at all times. Topping the list of most popular is the Knotty Blond, close to a pilsner in taste.

"My goal," Underwood notes, "is to create high-quality Northwest beers. For example, our IPA is hoppier than most and we're working toward making more extreme tasty beers."

Beers are served on two sides of a pub building that is designed to look like an old-fashioned livery stable. Walk in the main entrance and the family-friendly section is to your left. The over-21 pub, complete with pool table and view of the brewing operations, is to the right. An outdoor patio seats 70 during the warm months and is dog-friendly.

A Mountain Biker's Hot Spot

Not far from the patio area is a planned-for trail that will connect Three Creeks Brewing directly to the Peterson Ridge trail system. This will greatly enhance the ease of getting to and from the trails and the start of the Sisters Stampede Mountain Bike Race that the brewery inaugurated in 2010.

Ride the trails, hike the trails, run the trails, and then enjoy the pub at the end of the adventure. It doesn't get much better than that in active Central Oregon.

"My goal is to create high-quality Northwest beers."

Location	**Brewery and Brewpub**
	721 Desperado Court
	Sisters, OR 97759
Established	2008
Founder/Owner	Wade Underwood
Brewmaster(s)	Pat Shea
Web site	www.threecreeksbrewing.com
Phone	541.549.1963
Standard Beers	Knotty Blonde
	Anvil Amber
	Stonefly Rye
	Firestorm Red
	Hoodoo Voodoo
	Old Prospector
Seasonal Beers	Rudolph's Imperial Red
	and various other seasonal
	beers

Breweries in the Works

GoodLife Brewing Company

1355 SW Commerce Ave
Bend, OR 97702

Curt Plants, Ty Barnett, Pratt Rather

Take a successful brewery start-up specialist (Pratt Rather), a brewer (Curt Plants) with deep Bend roots and international craft brewing training, and a restaurant business pro (Ty Barnett) and you have the GoodLife Brewing Company (formerly Noble Brewing) team. Located in Bend's Century Center, GoodLife combines a 30-barrel capacity brewing operation with a beer hall/tasting room. What's being brewed on one side of the building can be tasted in a spacious room on the other side with its three roll-up doors that let the outside in. Inside or out, patrons can enjoy a unique menu of appetizers, salads, and pasties all created from locally sourced products while sampling beers including the Mountain Rescue Pale Ale, Pass Stout, and other beer varieties with an adventurous flair. "Balanced beers with aroma and flavor" is what the brewery's managing partners strive for while pointing out that one of their mottoes is "tap into the GoodLife."

Old Mill Brew Wërks

384 SW Upper Terrace Drive
Bend, OR 97702

David & Teri Love

When David Love first considered forming a Bend home brewers cooperative, he quickly discovered that to do so required having a brewing facility. That led to the October 2010 opening of Brew Wërks in Bend's Old Mill District. Serving food and harder-to-find craft beers in the pub, the brewery also became a place where home brewers could create their own beers with the prospect of having them featured on tap. In January 2011, Brew Wërks debuted its own Irreverance IPA followed by the Alterior Motive Altbier. A Kölsch was added in March. From the outset, Love and his wife Teri and brewmaker Justin James, have offered patrons a comfortable (TV-free) German Bierstube atmosphere. "Our goal," says Love," is to promote German style lagers and ales. Beers you'd normally find in Cologne and Düsseldorf, not in Bend or Redmond."

Glossary of Beer Terms

Short, but oh so informative

Ale: Most often dark amber in color, ales are top-fermented and are full of hoppiness (lots of hops but also a secondary meaning as in happy to be drinking beer).

Altbier: A lightly hoppy German beer from the Düsseldorf area that is the closest thing we have today to beers of centuries ago.

Bitter: Well-hopped beers that have an acidic finish on the tongue.

Bock: We're talking strong beer from malt that's dark, sweet and heavy.

Cask Conditioned: Take a beer or ale and forget about filtering or pasteurizing it before putting it into a cask to age in a cool basement or some other dark scary place.

Fermentation: Rather than subject you to a million words on popular fermentation processes, we offer the following:

- **Top** (warm) fermenting: The way ales are made at warmer temperatures where the yeast forms a foam on top of the beer being brewed.

- **Bottom** (cool) fermenting: This process requires cool temperatures and the yeast tends to collect at the bottom of the brewing vat.

Growler: Back before glass containers were commonplace, lads used to head down to the local pub with galvanized, lidded pails to get some take-home beer. Apparently on the return journey, the sloshing beer let off a lot of carbon dioxide which would bubble up against the pail's lid making a "growling" sound.

Hefeweizen: Literally "yeast wheat" in German, this effervescent beer gets its taste as the yeast works in the bottle leaving a bit of cloudiness from sediment.

IPA: Leave it to the thirsty Brits living in India to come up with a high alcohol beer with plenty of hops that could stand weeks of boat travel from England to the Raj.

Kölsch: Back to Germany, where, in the area around Cologne, this top-fermented, golden pale, fruity beer is king.

Lager: This crisp, golden beer made its way to the U.S. with German immigrants who immediately went in search of caves to store their creations. Lager literally means "storage" in German.

Pilsner: The world's most popular beer style, this golden colored, crisp, lager beer was first brewed by the Bürgerliches Brauhaus in the Bohemian (Czech) town of Pilsen in 1842. Prior to its creation, beers were very cloudy and not very tasty looking.

Porter: Named for the workmen who hauled goods from wagons to marketplaces in London, porters are strong, bottom-fermented ales with roasted malt added during the brewing process.

Stout: We're talking big, top-fermented ales with full bodies that come in many flavors and always with 6 to 7 percent alcohol content.

Imperial Stout: When the Russian tsars discovered British stout, they said: amp up the alcohol to 9 and 10 percent and ship us as much as you can, now. And we know the result of too much tsarist stout swilling.

The Bend Ale Trail™

Bend and Central Oregon are widely regarded as one of America's premier outdoor recreation playgrounds. After-play hours, there are a number of high-quality craft brewers and brewpubs to visit and enjoy. Seven world-class craft breweries call Bend home and there's a brewery each in nearby Redmond and Sisters.

The Bend Ale Trail gives visitors and locals alike a glimpse into the unique craft brewery culture of Central Oregon. Learn about the cutting-edge brewing techniques, meet the artisan brewers, and experience the diversity of styles, art and taste that differentiate each of our region's breweries.

Ready for a trek along the Bend Ale Trail? Use the Bend Ale Trail map to discover all of Central Oregon's great brewers and brewpubs. Be sure to collect a stamp as you visit each brewery because the completed passport is worth something in the end. Once you complete your passport, stop by the Visit Bend Welcome Center to get your prize. No purchase is required.

The Bend Ale Trail map, including the Passport, can be found at breweries and brewpubs, the Visit Bend Welcome Center, and online at bendaletrail.com.

Now, how do you get around the Bend Ale Trail? The Bend Ale Trail is definitely walk-able or bike-able, but you can also choose from one of these organized shuttle tour options:

- GETIT Shuttle
- The Bend Brew Bus
- The Cycle Pub of Bend
- Horse-drawn wagon beer tour

Visit bendaletrail.com for more details on getting around the trail.

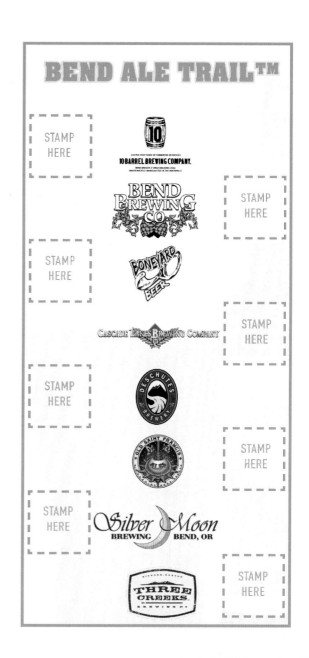

About the Authors

André Bartels

A German native, André Bartels grew up in a culture that honors beer and beer making. Since coming to the U.S. and settling in Bend, he's made an exhaustive search for the best craft brews.

Bob Woodward

Former Mayor (1997-1999) and three-decade Bend resident, Bob Woodward does his share in keeping Bend's per-capita beer consumption up.